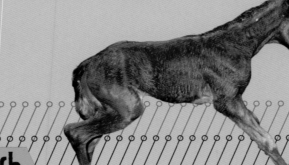

Start TO Finish
Second Series

Nature's Cycles

FROM Foal TO Horse

ROBIN NELSON

LERNER PUBLICATIONS COMPANY · Minneapolis

Photo Acknowledgments

The images in this book are used with the permission of: © Jane Burton/naturepl.com, pp. 1, 7, 9, 11; © Four Oaks/Shutterstock Images, p. 3; © Juniors Bildarchiv/Photolibrary, p. 5; © hunta/Shutterstock Images, p. 13; © William Muñoz, p. 15; © iStockphoto.com/John Rich, p. 17; © Claudia Steininger/Shutterstock Images, p. 19; © iStockphoto.com/Angela Medler, p. 21; © Zuzule/Shutterstock Images, p. 23.

Front cover: © pirita/Shutterstock Images.

Lerner Publications Company
A division of Lerner Publishing Group, Inc.
241 First Avenue North
Minneapolis, MN 55401 U.S.A.

Website address: www.lernerbooks.com

Main body text set in Arta Std Book 20/26.
Typeface provided by International Typeface Corp.

Library of Congress Cataloging-in-Publication Data

Nelson, Robin, 1971–
      From foal to horse / by Robin Nelson.
           p.   cm. — (Start to finish, second series. Nature's cycles)
      Includes index.
      ISBN 978-0-7613-8672-8 (lib. bdg. : alk. paper)
      1. Foals—Juvenile literature. 2. Horses—Juvenile literature. I. Title.
SF302.N453 2012
636.1—dc23   2011024564

Manufactured in the United States of America
1 – DP – 12/31/11

TABLE OF Contents

Look! A horse!

How does a horse grow?

A farmer raises horses.

Most horses are raised on farms. Farmers take care of the horses. A male horse is called a **stallion**. A female horse is called a **mare**. This mare has a baby horse growing inside her body.

A baby horse is born.

A baby horse is ready to be born after eleven months. The farmer helps the mare give birth. The baby horse is called a **foal** after it is born.

The foal stands up.

The foal tries to stand a few minutes after it is born. Its long legs are weak. The foal must try a few times before it is strong enough to stand on its own.

The mare cleans her foal.

The mare licks her foal to clean it. Then the mare and the foal sniff each other. They learn each other's smell.

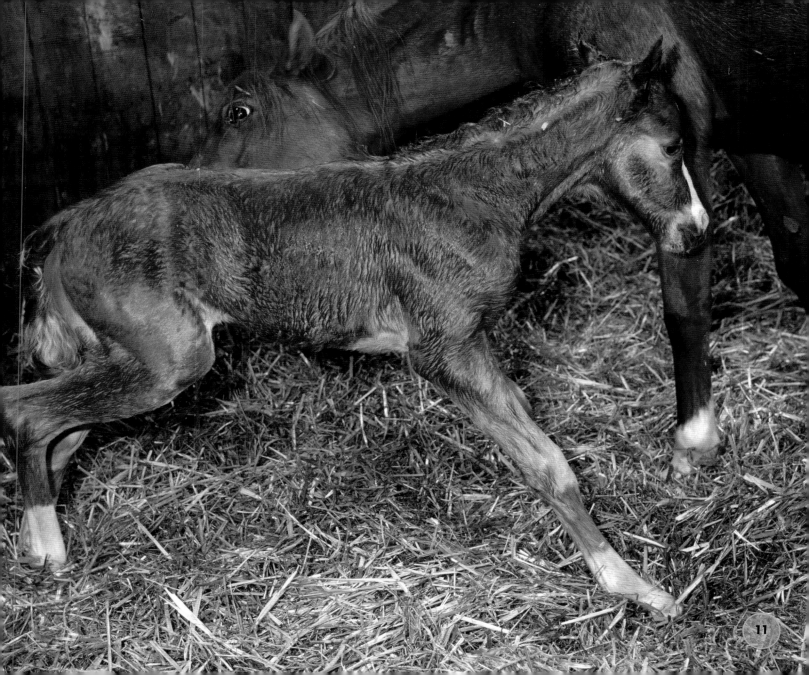

The foal drinks milk.

The foal **nurses** by drinking milk from the mare. The mare's milk helps the foal stay healthy and grow.

The foal gets stronger.

The foal plays with the other foals on the farm. The foals run and jump together. They grow strong and fast.

The foal starts to eat grass.

The foal starts to eat grass when it is about one month old. It also eats hay, corn, and oats that the farmer feeds it. The foal still nurses too.

The foal stops nursing.

The foal stops nursing when it is six months old. It no longer lives with its mother. The foal eats food instead of drinking milk.

The foal becomes a yearling.

The foal is called a yearling when it is one year old. It is much bigger than a newborn foal. But the yearling is not done growing yet.

The yearling grows up.

A male yearling is called a stallion when he is three years old. A female yearling is called a mare when she is three years old. The horse in this picture is a mare. She has grown from foal to horse!

Glossary

foal (FOHL): a horse that is less than one year old

mare (MAYR): an adult female horse

nurses (NUR-sihz): drinks milk from a mother's body

stallion (STAL-yuhn): an adult male horse

yearling (YEER-ling): a horse that is one to three years old

Index